ATLAS OF WORLD FAITHS

SIKHISM

Jane Bingham

A+

Smart Apple Media

This book has been published in cooperation with
Arcturus Publishing Limited.

The right of Jane Bingham to be identified as the author
of this work has been asserted by her in accordance with
the Copyright, Designs and Patents Act 1988.

Series concept: Alex Woolf
Editor and picture researcher: Alex Woolf
Designer: Simon Borrough
Cartography: Encompass Graphics
Consultant: Douglas G. Heming

Picture credits:
Corbis: 32 (Bettmann), 35 (Kapoor Baldev/Sygma),
37 (Kapoor Baldev/Sygma), 39 (Buddy Mays).
Hulton Archive/Getty Images: 28–29.
World Religions Photo Library: 4 (Christine Osborne), 6
(Christine Osborne), 9 (Christine Osborne), 11
(Christine Osborne), 13 (Prem Kapoor), 15 (Christine
Osborne), 16 (Prem Kapoor), 18 (Christine Osborne),
20 (Christine Osborne), cover and 22 (Christine
Osborne), 25 (Prem Kapoor), 27 (Christine Osborne),
31 (Christine Osborne).

Library of Congress Cataloging-in-Publication Data

Bingham, Jane.
Sikhism / by Jane Bingham.
p. cm.—(Atlas of world faiths)
Includes index.
ISBN 978-1-59920-059-0
1. Sikhism—History—Juvenile literature. I. Title. II.
Series.

BL2017.6.B56 2007
294.609—dc22   2007007535

9 8 7 6 5 4 3 2 1

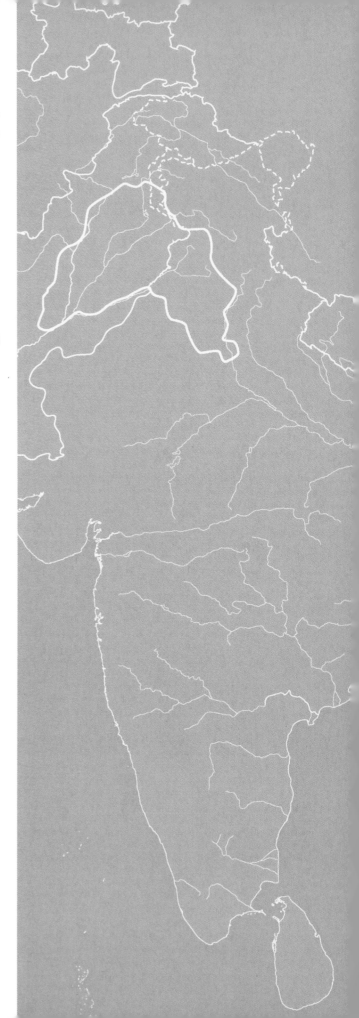

CONTENTS

CHAPTER 1:
THE ORIGINS OF SIKHISM

The Sikh religion began in India at the end of the fifteenth century. It was founded by a great teacher named Guru Nanak. Nanak lived in Punjab, a fertile region of northwestern India between the Himalaya Mountains and the Ganges River. In the fifteenth century, the Punjab region was an important center of Hinduism, but it was controlled by Muslim rulers. This meant that Nanak grew up in close contact with two great religions.

The area where Sikhism began was originally Hindu, but in the eleventh century it was invaded by Muslims. This minaret (prayer tower) was built in Delhi to celebrate a Muslim victory over the Hindus. Work began on the tower, known as the Qutub Minar, in 1193.

Guru Nanak Nanak was born in 1469 in the Punjabi village of Talwandi. Talwandi is about 50 miles (80 km) southwest of the city of Lahore and is now in Pakistan. It has been renamed Nankana Sahib, which means "the Lord Nanak," in honor of the founder of the Sikh faith.

Nanak's family was Hindu, but his father managed the accounts of a local Muslim landlord.

From an early age, Nanak studied the religions of Hinduism and Islam. He also spent a lot of time on his own, thinking about the nature of God. Later, he founded a new religion based on everything that he had learned. Because of his great wisdom, Nanak was given the title "guru," which means "teacher" in the ancient Indian language, Sanskrit.

Muslim rule At the time Nanak was born, Hinduism had been the dominant religion in India for at least 3,500 years. But Muslims had ruled northern India for the previous 500 years. Since 1000 CE, there had been three waves of Muslim invaders, who each took turns ruling the Indian people. Around the year 1000, Muslim warriors from Afghanistan came over the mountains into India, killing hundreds of Indians and destroying their temples. In the 1200s, bands of Muslim Turks marched through Punjab and seized control of the city of Delhi. Turkish sultans ruled most of India for the next 150 years. Then, in the fourteenth century, a new Afghan leader named Timur launched a savage attack on northern India.

During Nanak's lifetime, northern India was ruled by Afghan kings, known as the Lodhis. (See the map on page 7 for the extent of the Lodhi kingdom.) This was a fairly peaceful time for the Punjab region, but many Hindus still resented their Muslim conquerors. Nanak would later teach his followers to rise above religious hatred, saying that Sikhs must treat everyone with respect, regardless of their religion.

Studying Islam As Nanak grew up, he observed Muslims practicing their religion. He discussed Islamic beliefs with Muslim scholars and studied their holy book, the Qur'an. Nanak was especially interested in Sufism, a branch of Islam that had begun in Persia (present-day

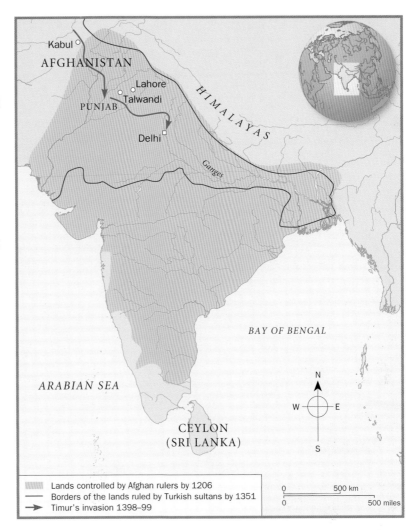

A map of India showing Muslim invasions between the twelfth and fourteenth centuries.

Legend:
- Lands controlled by Afghan rulers by 1206
- Borders of the lands ruled by Turkish sultans by 1351
- Timur's invasion 1398–99

Iran). Sufis lead a very simple life and meditate on the nature of God. Nanak admired the mystical nature of the Sufis. He tried to achieve a similar state of understanding through his religious practices.

ONE GOD

Although he disagreed with many Muslim teachings, Nanak was impressed by the Muslim belief in a single God. He found this belief much more convincing than the Hindus' devotion to many gods. Sikhs believe in a single, supreme God. During their services, they chant the words *Ik Onkar*, which mean, "One God."

A divided society

Guru Nanak had a comfortable childhood. But the Hindu society in which he grew up was full of conflict. It was divided into kingdoms that often went to war against each other. Within these kingdoms were powerful family groups, or clans, and these different groups often engaged in bitter local feuds. Nanak decided that when he grew up, he must try to do something to stop these conflicts.

The caste system

In the fifteenth century, Hindu society was not just divided into clans, it was also ruled by the rigid caste system. This ancient system divided people into four main castes, or classes. The highest caste was the Brahmans, who were priests and scholars. Next came the Kshatriyas, who were the descendants of warriors and kings. The third class was the Vaisyas, who traditionally worked as merchants and farmers. The lowest caste was the workers, known as the Sudras. Below all these castes was a group called the "untouchables." They did the jobs that none of the other castes were expected to do. The untouchables were not allowed to mix with people of other castes.

Rejecting caste

Nanak's family belonged to the Kshatriya, or warrior caste, but he rejected this way of dividing and judging people. When he was 11 years old, Nanak refused to take part in the ceremony to welcome him to his caste. Instead of accepting the *janeu*, a sacred thread that showed he was a Ksatriya, he challenged the priest who offered it to him. In front of his whole family, Nanak asked the question: shouldn't people earn respect through their actions, rather than by wearing a sacred thread? This was the start of Nanak's lifelong commitment to the equality of all people.

Studying Hinduism

Nanak was educated as a Hindu and learned all the teachings of his faith. He attended school where he was taught by priests, and he also talked to wandering Hindu holy men. One branch of Hinduism had a special appeal for Nanak. This was the bhakti movement, which had developed in the thirteenth century. Bhaktis ignore caste and concentrate on the individual's relationship with a personal god. Later, Guru Nanak adopted the idea of a personal god in his hymns. However, the Sikh god does not take a human form, unlike the bhakti god.

The birthplace of Guru Nanak in Talwandi has become a Sikh shrine. Many Sikhs make a pilgrimage to worship there.

EVERYONE IS EQUAL

Sikhs believe that all human beings are equal—male and female, young and old, rich and poor. This is because they believe that all people are equally loved by God.

Though they say there are four castes,
One God created all men
All men are molded of the same clay.
The Great Potter has merely varied their shapes.

Hymn from the Sikhs' holy book, the Guru Granth Sahib

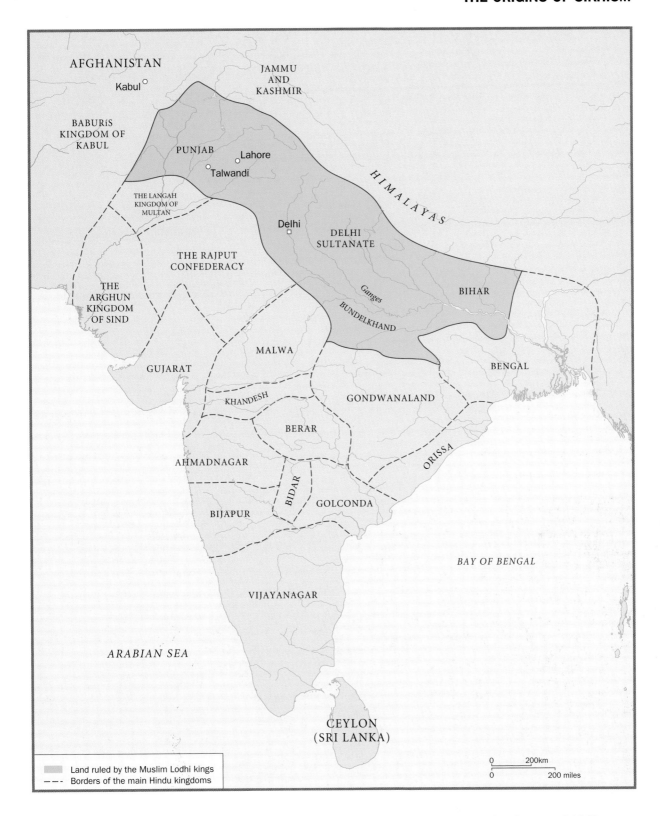

AFGHANISTAN

Kabul ○

JAMMU AND KASHMIR

BABUR'S KINGDOM OF KABUL

PUNJAB

Lahore ○

Talwandi ○

THE LANGAH KINGDOM OF MULTAN

Delhi □

DELHI SULTANATE

HIMALAYAS

THE RAJPUT CONFEDERACY

THE ARGHUN KINGDOM OF SIND

Ganges

BIHAR

BUNDELKHAND

GUJARAT

MALWA

KHANDESH

GONDWANALAND

BENGAL

BERAR

AHMADNAGAR

BIDAR

ORISSA

BIJAPUR

GOLCONDA

BAY OF BENGAL

VIJAYANAGAR

ARABIAN SEA

CEYLON (SRI LANKA)

Land ruled by the Muslim Lodhi kings
- - - Borders of the main Hindu kingdoms

0 ____ 200km
0 ____ 200 miles

A map of India around 1460, showing the main Hindu kingdoms and the Muslim Lodhi lands.

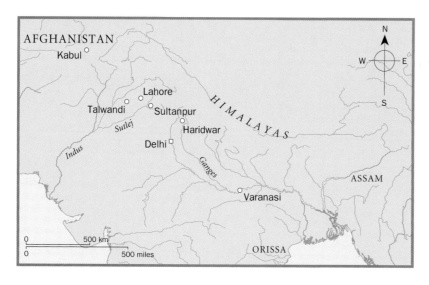

A map of important places in Guru Nanak's early life.

Guru Nanak's early life

There are many stories about the early life of Guru Nanak, and all of them illustrate the fact that he was a remarkable child. One story tells how the infant Nanak was born with a powerful sense of holiness. This was immediately recognized both by the Muslim midwife and the Hindu priest who were present at Nanak's birth. The priest prepared a horoscope for the boy, predicting that Hindus and Muslims alike would recognize Nanak as a great thinker and teacher.

Once he reached school age, Nanak astonished all of his teachers with his wisdom and understanding. At the age of seven he started composing hymns that expressed his own beliefs. Like all of his fellow students, Nanak spoke Punjabi, which was a spoken language without any written form. However, by the time he was a teenager Nanak had mastered three written languages. He could write fluently in Sanskrit, the ancient language of the Hindu texts. He could also read and write Arabic and Persian, the languages of Islam.

Life in Sultanpur

When he was about 16 years old, Nanak left the village of Talwandi and set off for Sultanpur, a small town close to the Sutlej River. Nanak's married sister lived in Sultanpur and she found work for her brother as a tax collector for a local Muslim ruler. Over the next eight years, Nanak also devoted himself to religious studies and began to attract a group of followers. During this time, Nanak married a Hindu girl, Sulakhni, and had two sons. Meanwhile, his fame was spreading. A large group of followers arrived in Sultanpur to join with Nanak in his hymns, prayers, and contemplation.

Nanak's travels

After eight years in Sultanpur, Nanak became restless. He decided it was time to meet new people and to learn what they looked for in their faith. So, in the summer of 1496, he set off on a series of journeys.

It is impossible to be certain exactly where Nanak went, but most accounts agree that he first headed east to the ancient cities of Haridwar and Varanasi. Then, he traveled widely in the Assam and Orissa regions in northern India. These were all holy Hindu places, with magnificent shrines and libraries. Here, Nanak shared ideas with pilgrims, scholars, and mystics.

After he left the north, stories say that Nanak visited the great Hindu kingdoms of southern India. While he was in the south, it is said that he also traveled to the island of Ceylon (present-day Sri Lanka), where the Buddhist religion was practiced.

As he traveled through India, Nanak spread his ideas. Sometimes Nanak preached in a Hindu temple, sometimes in a mosque, and sometimes in the open air. He also visited people's houses and joined them in singing the hymns he had composed.

OFFERINGS TO GOD

A story is told about a meeting in the Hindu city of Haridwar. Here, a group of Hindu priests explained their practice of sacrificing animals for their gods to Nanak. He listened carefully, then responded: "The sacrifices . . . of this age should consist in giving food to those who repeat God's name and practice humility."

This temple in Pancha Sahib, close to Lahore, was built in memory of Guru Nanak. The Guru stayed here for a while, and it is believed that he left his handprint close to the tank of holy water.

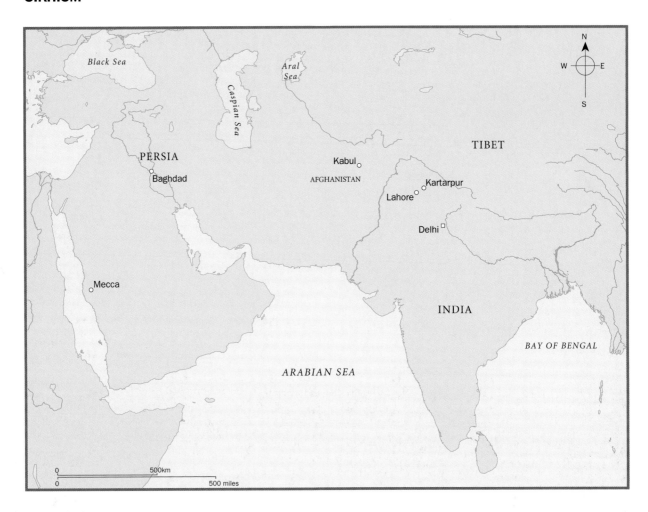

A map showing places visited by Guru Nanak during his later travels.

Later journeys

Later in his life, Guru Nanak made other journeys in search of greater understanding. According to one story, Nanak traveled to the Muslim cities of Kabul (in Afghanistan), Mecca (in present-day Saudi Arabia), and Baghdad (in present-day Iraq). He may also have visited the Buddhist monasteries in Tibet. Wherever he went, he observed the practices of the different religions. He spoke to ordinary worshippers, studied holy texts, and discussed ideas with scholars.

Time to reflect

After his travels, Guru Nanak returned to Punjab. There he found a peaceful spot on the Ravi River, north of Lahore, and established the village of Kartarpur. Nanak spent the last 15 years of his life at Kartarpur, trying to form a new religion from the essential parts of everything he had learned. In these peaceful years, Guru Nanak wrote a collection of hymns that became the basis of the new faith.

Guru Nanak's message

In his hymns, Guru Nanak taught that there is only one God and that all human beings are equal. He encouraged his followers to devote their lives to God. He also taught that people should be prepared to work hard in the service of God and their fellow human beings.

The first Sikhs

Many followers flocked to Kartarpur to be close to Guru Nanak. These people became known as "sikhs," which comes from the Sanskrit word for "follower." Sikhs were from a range of castes and faiths. Many were farmers, some had belonged to the warrior caste, while others came from Muslim families. One of Guru Nanak's closest companions was a Muslim named Mardana. He abandoned his Muslim faith to join Nanak early in his travels and accompanied the guru for the rest of his life.

At Kartarpur, Nanak started a practice of sharing a meal with anyone who came to hear him preach. After the service, everybody joined in a shared meal, known as the *langar*, rejecting the caste system that did not allow members of different castes to eat together.

A new language When Guru Nanak preached to his followers, he used the local language of Punjabi. However, this was just a spoken language. Nanak was faced with the problem of what language to use for his written texts. He did not want to use Sanskrit, the holy language of the Hindus, or Arabic or Persian, the languages of Islam. So he decided to create a new written language based on Punjabi. This language is called Gurmukhi, which means "from the guru's mouth." It is still used today for all Sikh holy texts.

GURU NANAK'S HYMNS

Guru Nanak wrote 974 hymns. These were later collected in the Sikh holy book, the Guru Granth Sahib. Some of Guru Nanak's hymns are read or sung at all Sikh services. His most famous hymn is the Mool Mantra, which Sikhs are supposed to say every day. It begins with the following words: *There is Only One God. He is all that is. He is the creator of all things, and he is everywhere.*

A Sikh boy reads from the Sikh holy book, the Guru Granth Sahib. Like all Sikh texts, it is written in the Gurmukhi script, a language created by Guru Nanak.

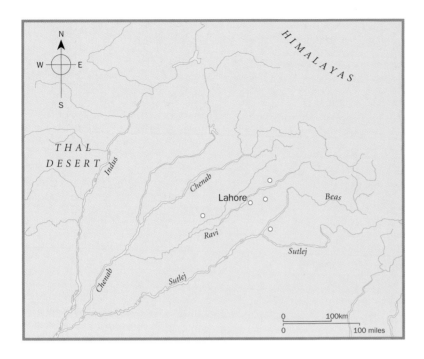

A map of the Sikh heartland around 1580.

Guru Angad

Guru Nanak died in 1539, but before his death, he chose a new teacher to continue his work. This was Guru Angad, a well educated man who lived in the small village of Khadur, south of Amritsar, near the Beas River. Guru Angad spent the next 13 years teaching the Sikh religion. He collected all of Guru Nanak's hymns into a book and also added 62 new hymns of his own.

Guru Angad set up schools to teach young people to read and write Gurmukhi. He also encouraged his followers to take part in sports. He taught the Sikhs that both a healthy mind and body were pleasing to God.

Guru Amar Das

Guru Angad chose Amar Das, one of his most devoted followers, to be the third guru. Guru Amar Das was the leader of the Sikhs from 1552 to 1574. During his time as guru, he sent his followers all over Punjab to spread the faith. He also established a center for Sikhs at Goindwal, on the banks of the Beas River. Guru Amar Das held celebrations at Goindwal three times a year and encouraged Sikhs from all over Punjab to join him.

Guru Amar Das also introduced the communal eating hall, known as a langar hall. This was a place where everyone shared a simple meal together. Anyone who came to visit Guru Amar Das would eat with him in the langar hall.

The temple at Amritsar

Before he died, Guru Amar Das chose a site for a special Sikh temple. He decided that the temple should be built at the village of Amritsar. The site was chosen for its beautiful location on the shores of a lake, surrounded by forests.

In 1574, Guru Ram Das became the fourth guru. He was a devoted Sikh and the husband of the third guru's younger daughter. Guru Ram Das led the Sikhs for the next seven years. During this time, he devoted himself to building the temple at Amritsar.

In 1581, Guru Ram Das was succeeded by his son, Guru Arjan, and from then on, gurus usually chose their sons to succeed them. Guru Arjan led the Sikhs until 1606 and completed the task of building the temple at Amritsar. This stunning temple, constructed on an island, later became known as the Golden Temple.

THE DUTY OF *SEWA*

The gurus did not merely plan the layout of the temple at Amritsar, they also helped with the physical tasks of digging and construction. Sikhs believe that they should serve God by performing simple physical tasks. The name for this service is *sewa*. By performing sewa, Sikhs show that they are all humble before God. Today, Sikhs fulfill the sewa duty by helping out in their temple. They take turns keeping the temple clean. They also cook and serve a simple meal for everyone to share in the langar hall.

A holy book Guru Arjan also compiled a holy book for the Sikhs. He collected the hymns of the first four gurus and added some new hymns of his own. He also chose some writings by Muslim and Hindu holy men. This holy book was known as the Adi Granth. In 1604, Guru Arjan installed the original copy of Adi Granth in a place of honor in the temple at Amritsar.

The Golden Temple at Amritsar is part of a complex of religious buildings (see its floor plan on page 36). The temple is known as the Harmandir Sahib and is the holiest part of the complex.

CHAPTER 2:
THE SIKHS AND THE MOGULS

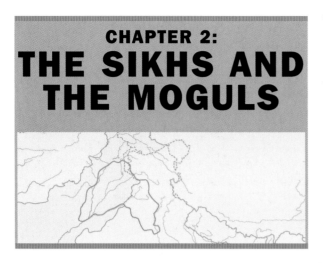

The Mogul Empire By the 1600s, northern India had been ruled by the Moguls for almost a century. The Moguls were Muslims from Afghanistan who had seized control of Delhi in 1526. Their leader, Babur, declared himself the first Mogul emperor, and his grandson, Akbar, built a vast empire that covered northern India.

Akbar was a wise and tolerant ruler, who was interested in learning about all religions. However, his son, Jahangir, was a very different man. Jahangir was determined to make Islam the only religion of the Mogul Empire, and he saw the Sikhs as his enemies.

Less than two years after the Adi Granth was installed at Amritsar, Guru Arjan was arrested by the Mogul emperor Jahangir. This marked the beginning of a long and bitter battle between the Moguls and the Sikhs.

A shocking death Emperor Jahangir was a cruel man who made many enemies; one of his most determined enemies was his oldest son, Ksuru. In 1606, Ksuru rose up in revolt against his father. Jahangir defeated the rebellion and inflicted violent punishments on all of his son's supporters. Unfortunately, Ksuru had once met Guru Arjan, so Jahangir decided that the guru was involved in his son's revolt. Jahangir ordered that the holy man be arrested and tortured to death.

Guru Arjan's death was terrible. He was seated on a hot iron plate and burning sand was poured on him. Then he was immersed in near-boiling water, and finally, he was drowned in the Ravi River. However, the guru did not protest this torture. Later, his Sufi friend Mian Mir recorded some of the guru's last words: "I bear all this torture to set an example to the teachers of the True Name, that they may not lose patience or complain to God in their sufferings."

Lahore

Delhi

Agra

HIMALAYAS

BAY OF BENGAL

N

W   E

S

ARABIAN SEA

0   500 km
0   500 miles

The Mogul Empire in 1600

The Mogul Empire in 1600, showing the major centers of Muslim rule.

A painting of Guru Arjan, the fifth guru. After his tragic death, many Sikhs decided that they must fight to defend their religion.

A turning point The torture and death of Guru Arjan marked a dramatic turning point in Sikh history. His followers responded to the news of their leader's death with rage. This shocking incident changed Sikhism from a peaceful religious faith into a warrior movement. It was the start of 150 years of warfare against the Moguls and other Islamic forces.

BABUR, AKBAR, AND THE SIKHS

The cruel act of Emperor Jahangir was a tragedy for the Sikhs and the Moguls. Until that time, the Moguls had a good relationship with the Sikhs. Emperor Babur met Guru Nanak and talked to him about religion. Emperor Akbar visited Guru Amar Das at Goindwal and shared a meal with him. Akbar also offered Guru Ram Das a gift of land for the Sikh temple he was planning to build.

Sikhs arrive to celebrate a festival at Anandpur Sahib. This important temple was built near Kiratpur, in memory of Guru Hargobind.

Guru Hargobind Guru Hargobind was the eldest son of Guru Arjan. He was only 11 years old when he succeeded his father in 1606, but he immediately began to build an army to fight the Moguls.

In 1628, the Sikhs and the Moguls clashed for the first time. The battle, which was fought close to Amritsar, lasted for two days, and the Mogul army was defeated. Hargobind realized that if he stayed in Amritsar, the temple would be in danger, so he left the holy city and went into the hills. He never saw Amritsar again.

Two more battles followed—at Lahira, in southern Punjab, in 1631 and at Kartarpur, near Amritsar, in 1634. Both ended in victory for the Sikhs. These victories increased the anger of the Moguls, and Guru Hargobind spent the rest of his life fighting off Mogul attacks.

Guru Hargobind lived a wandering life, visiting Sikhs all over the Punjab region. However, toward the end of his life, he settled in Kiratpur, in the foothills of the Himalayas. This later became the site of a famous Sikh temple known as Anandpur Sahib.

GURDWARAS

For most of his life, Guru Hargobind was traveling, but he needed a place to meet with other Sikhs. He established the gurdwara, a place for Sikhs to pray and read from their holy book. Gurdwara means "the door to the guru." Today, Sikhs all over the world meet in gurdwaras. A gurdwara does not need to be a grand building. It can be any place where the Sikh holy book is kept and where Sikhs meet to worship. Some gurdwaras are simply a special room in a Sikh's house.

Spreading the faith After Guru Hargobind's death in 1644, there was a period of relative calm. During this time, the seventh guru—Hargobind's grandson, Har Rai—took the opportunity to travel throughout the Punjab region, spreading the faith. While he was traveling, Guru Har Rai gave out free medicine to people who were sick, a practice continued by later gurus and their followers. In 1661, Guru Har Rai was succeeded by his five-year-old son. Unfortunately, the young Guru Har Krishan died of smallpox three years later.

Guru Tegh Bahadur

In 1664, Tegh Bahadur, the youngest of Guru Hargobind's sons, became the ninth guru. He traveled through northern India visiting Sikhs. On one of his journeys, Guru Tegh Bahadur visited Delhi, Mathura, Agra, Allahabad, Varanasi, Sasaram, and Gaya, all in northeastern India. This journey ended in Patna, east of Varanasi, where his son was born. Later, Guru Tegh Bahadur moved on to Dacca (in present-day Bangladesh), which already had a thriving Sikh community.

During his travels in northern India, Tegh Bahadur held discussions with followers of different religions. He talked to Hindu priests, Buddhist pilgrims, and Sufi mystics and tried to learn as much as he could about their beliefs and religious practices.

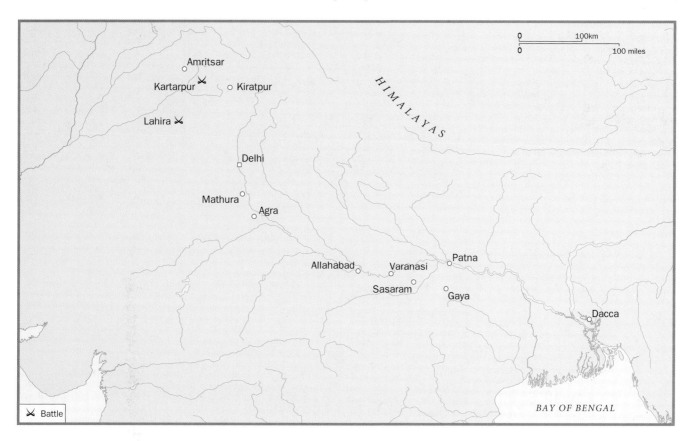

A map of important places in the lives of Guru Hargobind and Guru Tegh Bahadur.

This painting shows the origins of the Khalsa ceremony. Here, the five founders of the Khalsa gather in front of Guru Gobind Singh. One of them offers the sacred food of Karah Parshad to the guru.

A brave death In 1675, Guru Tegh Bahadur took a courageous stand against the Mogul emperor Aurangzeb. The emperor wanted to wipe out all religions except Islam, and when he gave orders for the Hindu temples of Kashmir to be destroyed, the Hindus appealed to Tegh Bahadur for help.

Guru Tegh Bahadur was determined to show that it was impossible to convert people to Islam by force, so he bravely set off on his own to meet the emperor.

Tegh Bahadur believed that he would be able to talk to Emperor Aurangzeb reasonably, but the emperor had other ideas. On his way to Delhi, Tegh Bahadur was arrested by the emperor's troops and brought to the city in an iron cage. For the next five days, he was tortured, but he refused to alter his religious beliefs. Eventually, Tegh Bahadur was beheaded. The spot where he died later became the site of a Sikh gurdwara called Sis Ganj.

Guru Gobind Singh

The tenth guru was Tegh Bahadur's son, Gobind Singh. He was only nine years old when his father died, but despite his youth, he was determined to defend the Sikh faith against its enemies. He established a strong base for the Sikhs in the mountain city of Anandpur, in the foothills of the Himalayas. He also studied many holy texts so that he could become a wise spiritual leader for his people.

In 1685, at the age of 19, Guru Gobind Singh took full charge of the Sikhs. In the early years of his leadership, he fought off several attacks on Anandpur. But in 1704, a powerful Mogul army forced the Sikhs to leave their city. Emperor Aurangzeb promised the Sikhs that they could leave Anandpur in safety, but he broke his word. Some of the emperor's troops attacked the retreating Sikhs, brutally killing men, women, and children.

After leaving Anandpur, Gobind Singh stayed in Dina, in present-day Pakistan. There he wrote two famous letters to Aurangzeb, blaming him for being untrue to the ideals of the Muslim religion. Surprisingly, these letters impressed Aurangzeb, who instructed his deputy to make peace with Gobind Singh. The events at Dina inspired the Sikhs, who rallied around their brave leader.

Guru Gobind Singh then moved to Talwandi Sabo, south of the Sutlej River. This peaceful place was later renamed Damdama Sahib. Here he completed the final version of the Sikh holy book, the Guru Granth Sahib. From then on, beautiful copies of the Guru Granth Sahib were created in Damdama Sahib.

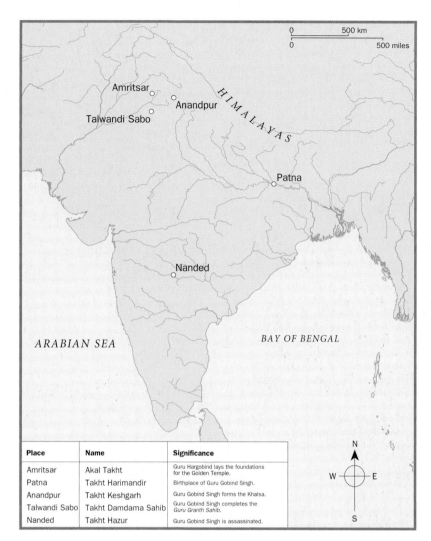

Place	Name	Significance
Amritsar	Akal Takht	Guru Hargobind lays the foundations for the Golden Temple.
Patna	Takht Harimandir	Birthplace of Guru Gobind Singh.
Anandpur	Takht Keshgarh	Guru Gobind Singh forms the Khalsa.
Talwandi Sabo	Takht Damdama Sahib	Guru Gobind Singh completes the *Guru Granth Sahib*.
Nanded	Takht Hazur	Guru Gobind Singh is assassinated.

The five Takhts: The Sikhs have built five Takhts (special temples) to mark the places where very important events took place in Sikh history. Four of them are connected with the life of Guru Gobind Singh.

THE FOUNDING OF THE KHALSA

In 1699, Guru Gobind Singh held a dramatic ceremony. He asked for volunteers who were prepared to die for their faith to step into his tent. Five men volunteered. They became the first members of a group of devout Sikhs known as the Khalsa. The Khalsa still continues today. Members of the Khalsa promise to obey the rules of the Sikh religion. They wear five symbols to remind them of their promise. See page 44 for a description of these symbols.

The Guru Granth Sahib is treated with great respect. It is placed on a cushion and fanned with a chowrie.

The end of the gurus

In 1707, Emperor Aurangzeb was succeeded by his son, Emperor Bahadur Shah I. The new emperor was much more reasonable than his father, so Guru Gobind Singh went to meet him in Agra, on the banks of the Yamuna River in northern India, and together they traveled south. Gobind Singh hoped that the emperor would allow the Sikhs to return to Anandpur. However, by the time they reached the town of Nanded, on the banks of the Godavari River, it was evident that they would not be able to return. So Guru Gobind Singh decided to settle in Nanded.

Many people flocked to Nanded to hear the teachings of Gobind Singh, and the town became a center for Sikhism in southern India. However, this peaceful time did not last long. In 1708, the local Muslim governor who was jealous of the power of Gobind Singh sent two assassins to murder him. The guru survived the attack, but he died soon after.

As he lay dying, Guru Gobind Singh announced that there should be no more gurus after him. He was aware that chaos could break out after his death as the scattered Sikhs quarreled about who should be their leader. Instead, Gobind Singh explained that the Sikhs should consider their holy book as their guru: for advice, they should turn to the Guru Granth Sahib.

Today, the Guru Granth Sahib is often called the "eleventh guru." Copies of the holy book are treated with great respect, as if they were living teachers. In gurdwaras, the book is the focus of Sikh worship. It usually rests on cushions on a platform and is covered by a canopy.

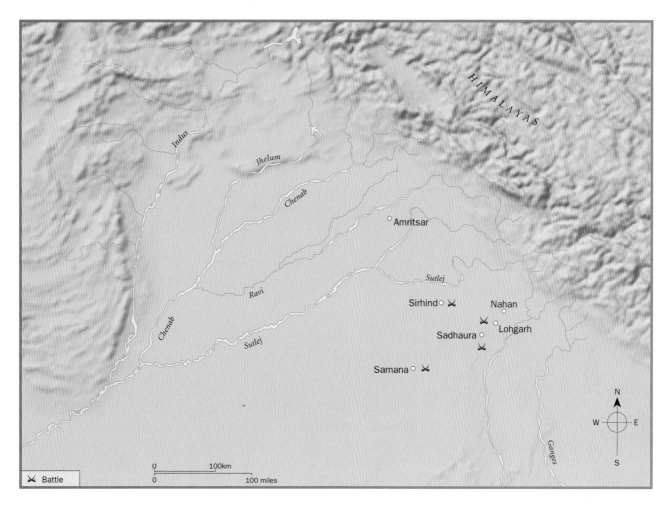

A map of important places in the military campaigns of Banda Singh.

Banda Singh In the months after the death of Guru Gobind Singh, Banda Singh emerged as the military leader of the Sikhs. He gathered a small army and marched toward the town of Samana in eastern Punjab. Banda's army captured Samana from the Mogul rulers and seized more than a dozen towns in eastern Punjab. Banda then chose the fortress at Mukhlispur, halfway between Sadhaura and Nahan, to be his base. He renamed the fortress Lohgarh and made it the capital of his new Sikh state. This was the first time the Sikhs claimed land as their own.

In August 1710, the Mogul emperor decided to strike back. A vast Muslim army descended on Punjab, and bloody battles were fought at Sadhaura, Sirhind, and Lohgarh. Over the next five years, Banda and his followers fought a determined campaign, winning cities from the Moguls but then losing them again. Eventually, the Sikhs were defeated in 1715. Banda was taken prisoner and hundreds of Sikhs were executed. But Banda had made a lasting difference in Punjab. Although the Moguls still controlled some important towns, the idea of a Sikh state had been born.

A time of chaos During the eighteenth century, the Sikhs had to deal with many enemies. They were persecuted by the Moguls and also faced invasions from Afghanistan. Between the years 1748 and 1764, Afghan armies invaded India eight times, and each time, they marched through Punjab, causing death and destruction. The most distressing attacks on the Sikhs were the Afghans' three separate attacks on the temple at Amritsar.

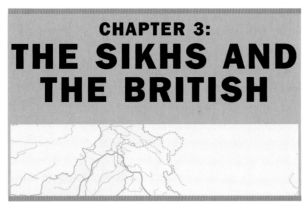

CHAPTER 3:
THE SIKHS AND THE BRITISH

Despite all of their troubles during the 1700s, the Sikhs were thriving by the 1800s. Since the death of Emperor Aurangzeb in 1707, the Mogul Empire had weakened. This allowed the Sikhs to gain control of large parts of eastern Punjab. They also controlled most of western Punjab (present-day Pakistan) and the mountainous areas north of Punjab.

The Sikhs ran their lands efficiently, and Sikh farmers produced a wide range of goods. During this period, the Sikhs also encouraged manufacturing and

The Sikh flag, known as the Nishan Sahib, plays a central part in all Sikh ceremonies. The symbol of the *khanda* at the center of the flag reminds Sikhs to be strong and brave and to fight for freedom and justice. These ideas have been very important in Sikh history.

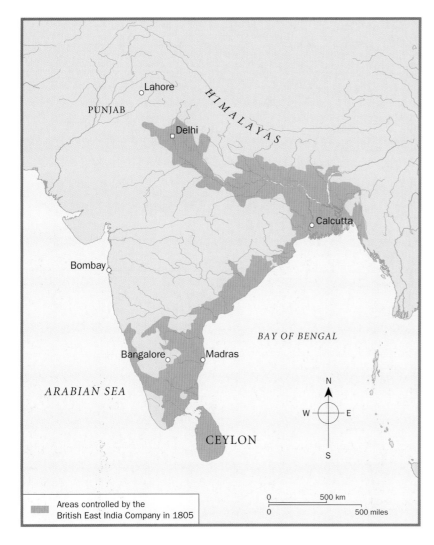

A map of India in 1805, showing the extent of British control.

Areas controlled by the British East India Company in 1805

trade, and their towns and cities grew. By the 1800s, the Sikhs were eager to conquer new lands. However, they were about to face a new challenge from the British East India Company.

The British in India

Traders from Europe had settled in India as early as the sixteenth century, and some trading companies became very powerful. In particular, the East India Company gradually gained control of large areas of India. By 1800, the East India Company was the real power behind the Mogul emperor, and the company maintained a large army to deal with any opposition. Later, the British did not hesitate to use this army against the Sikhs.

Ranjit Singh

Around 1800, a new Sikh leader emerged. Ranjit Singh was a brilliant horseman and warrior. He was also very ambitious. In 1799, at the age of 19, he led an army into Lahore and seized control of the city from the Muslims. Two years later, he was crowned maharaja (prince) of the Punjab. Ranjit Singh was the first Sikh leader to be crowned as a royal ruler, but this royal line did not last long after his death.

Ranjit Singh ruled Punjab efficiently and fairly. He treated the Muslims and Hindus in his kingdom well and chose several Muslims to hold important posts in his government. Meanwhile, he acquired more land for the Sikhs. Some territories were won in battle, and others were gained through trade. In less than ten years, Ranjit Singh had built a rich and powerful Sikh state in northwestern India. This made the British very nervous.

THE SIKH FLAG

Wherever the Sikhs conquered, they flew their flag. This flag, known as the Nishan Sahib, is still flown outside gurdwaras today. At the center of the flag is a symbol called the *khanda*. This symbol consists of a circle with a double-edged sword in its center and two curved swords on either side. The circle reminds Sikhs that there is only one God, who has no beginning and no end. The double-edged sword stands for freedom and justice. The two curved swords remind Sikhs to be strong, both in their daily life and in their beliefs.

The Treaty of Amritsar The British officials of the East India Company recognized that the Sikhs were valuable trading partners. Punjab was India's most productive area, both in terms of farm produce and manufactured goods, and the Sikhs governed the area effectively. However, the British were worried about Ranjit Singh's ambitions.

The British were not the only ones who felt threatened by Ranjit Singh. The Sikhs already controlled some territories south of the Sutlej River, and the local chiefs feared that their lands would be seized as well. In 1809, the British decided to support these leaders and take a stand against the young maharaja. They persuaded Ranjit Singh to sign the Treaty of Amritsar. In this agreement, Ranjit Singh agreed not to take any more territory south of the Sutlej River. In return, the British offered him their "perpetual friendship." Ranjit Singh agreed to the treaty because he needed to keep the British as his allies while he gained more land in the north.

Moving north After he had signed the Treaty of Amritsar, Ranjit Singh concentrated his efforts on the areas to the north and west of Punjab. As the Sikh army

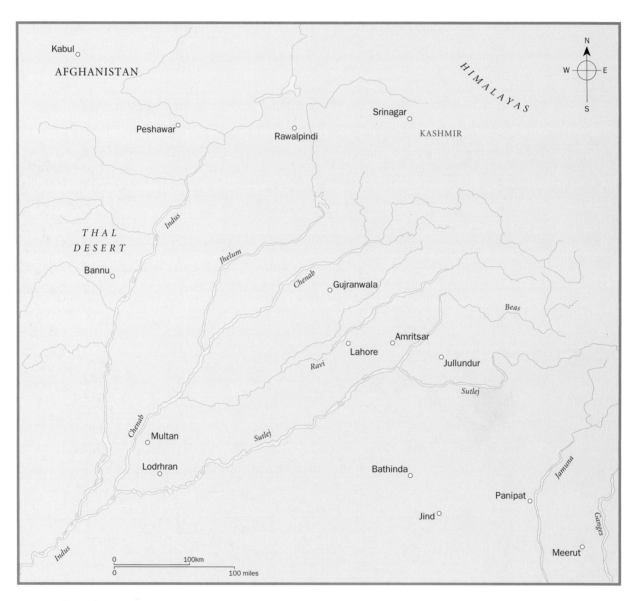

A map of the Sikh lands at the time of Ranjit Singh's death in 1839.

advanced on these regions, many local leaders appealed to the British for help. However, the British were obliged to ignore their pleas because of the terms of the Treaty of Amritsar.

Within the next 20 years, Ranjit Singh succeeded in driving the Afghans from many territories in the northwest. By 1839, the Sikhs had expanded their kingdom to include some rich northern regions, such as the kingdom of Kashmir and the areas around the cities of Peshawar and Kabul.

After Ranjit Singh

In 1839, Ranjit Singh died suddenly at the age of 58. During his lifetime, he had built up a great Sikh kingdom. But there was no one to take over upon his death. None of his sons had the qualities of a great leader, and over the next five years, the Sikh government in Lahore fell into chaos. In 1844, the British took advantage of the Sikhs' weakness. They arrived with a massive army and camped just south of the Sutlej River, waiting for their chance to attack the Sikhs.

Sikhs celebrate Hola Mohalla in Anandpur, Punjab. Today, this colorful ceremony reminds Sikhs of past battles for their faith.

HOLA MOHALLA

War has played a major part in Sikh history. Sikhs aspire to live peaceful lives, but they also believe that they should be prepared to fight for what they think is right. In the seventeenth century, Guru Gobind Singh introduced a spring festival known as Hola Mohalla. During this festival, Sikhs were trained to use weapons so that they could be prepared for war. Today, Sikhs still celebrate Hola Mohalla, but now they hold sporting events.

BRAVE WARRIORS

The British were impressed by the bravery of the Sikh soldiers they were fighting against. The commander of the British troops, Lord Hugh Gough, later described "the splendid gallantry of our fallen foe" and "the acts of heroism displayed by the Sikh army." Gough continued: "I could have wept to have witnessed the fearful slaughter of so devoted a body of men."

The First Anglo-Sikh War In November 1845, the British seized two Sikh villages near Ludhiana, south of the Sutlej River, claiming that they were sheltering criminals. When a Sikh army crossed the river to take back the villages, the British immediately declared war, claiming that the Sikhs had broken the terms of the Treaty of Amritsar. This was the start of the First Anglo-Sikh War.

In December 1845, the Sikhs fought the British at Mudki, where they were defeated, partly because the Sikh commander deserted his men. Three days later, the two sides met again at Ferozeshar. Here, the Sikhs fought fiercely for two days but were defeated again. In both of these battles, the Sikh soldiers fought bravely, but they were let down by their cowardly commanders, Lal Singh and Teja Singh.

The third battle of the war, at Aliwal, also ended in victory for the British, and more than 3,000 Sikhs were killed. In the final battle of the war, the Sikhs defended their stronghold at Sobraon. Again, the Sikh army suffered from poor leadership—their commanders made secret deals with the British—and the British army was victorious. The British marched straight to Lahore to negotiate their terms of victory with the Sikh government.

The Treaty of Lahore The Treaty of Lahore was signed in March 1846. Under its terms, all of the territories south of the Sutlej River were handed over to

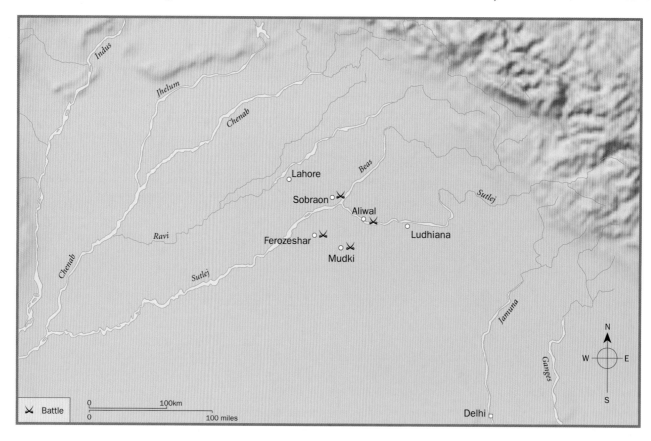

A map of important sites in the First Anglo-Sikh War (1845–46).

A Sikh artist's impression of a scene from the First Anglo-Sikh War. The war only lasted for a few months, but thousands of Sikhs were killed or injured.

the British. The British also gained the land between the Sutlej and Beas Rivers. This fertile region, known as Doaba, covers an area of 11,400 square miles (29,525 sq km).

A large portion of the Sikh kingdom went to Gulab Singh, the non-Sikh ruler of the northern kingdom of Jammu, who had made a secret alliance with the British during the war. As a reward for his cooperation, Gulab Singh was given a large stretch of land in northern Punjab. He also acquired the kingdom of Kashmir.

Kashmir had been given to the British in the Treaty of Lahore, but soon after signing the treaty, the British sold Kashmir to Gulab Singh.

The Treaty of Lahore left the Sikhs with less than two-thirds of their original kingdom. The Sikhs also had to agree to dramatically reduce their army and pay an annual sum to the British. Turn to the map on page 30 to see how the Sikh lands were divided.

The British take control

After the First Anglo-Sikh War, British troops stayed in Lahore. The Sikh government was in chaos, and the maharaja, Dalip Singh, was only eight years old. Taking advantage of the Sikhs' weakness, the British announced that they would govern the Sikh lands until Maharaja Dalip Singh came of age. This was greatly opposed by the Sikhs.

The Multan revolt

In April 1848, a riot broke out at Multan in southern Punjab. Trouble began when the British tried to replace a local ruler with a British governor. This attempt was resisted by the Sikhs, and two British officers were killed. In the chaos that followed, British troops marched on Multan, and the Sikhs united to oppose them. Eventually a Sikh army was formed, under the leadership of Sher Singh. The British decided to take serious action and they advanced on Multan with a large army. This was the start of the Second Anglo-Sikh War.

The Second Anglo-Sikh War

The first battle of the war was fought at Ramnagar, near the Chenab River, in November 1848. The Sikhs were greatly outnumbered, but they managed to defeat the British. Another battle followed at Sadulpur, a few miles up the Chenab River, but this time there was no obvious winner. However, in January 1849, the Sikhs won a clear victory at Chillianwala, near the Jhelum River. This left the British shocked and alarmed.

The British gathered their forces for the next battle, and in February 1849, an expanded British army faced the Sikhs at Gujrat, north of Sadulpur. The British had a force of around 68,000 soldiers, while the Sikhs had only 20,000. After two hours of fighting, it was clear that the British were winning, and the Sikhs retreated to the town of Rawalpindi, about 100 miles (160 km) north. In March 1849, the Sikhs surrendered Rawalpindi to the British, and the Second Anglo-Sikh War came to an end.

The British and the maharani

In the months before the Second Anglo-Sikh War, the British decided that Maharani Jind Kaur, the mother of the young Maharaja Dalip Singh, was a threat to British rule. The maharani had a strong personality, as well as many powerful friends who were prepared to fight for her and her son. The British were afraid that she was too powerful, so they sent her into exile. Maharani Jind Kaur was forced to live in the city of Varanasi, in British-controlled India. Her fortune was greatly reduced and most of her jewelry was confiscated. This humiliating treatment of the mother of their ruler enraged the Sikhs.

Sikh and British soldiers engage in fierce combat at the Battle of Chillianwala (1849). The battle ended in victory for the Sikhs.

A map of important sites in the
Second Anglo-Sikh War (1848–49).

THE KOH-I-NOOR DIAMOND

One of the greatest treasures owned by the young Maharaja Dalip Singh was the famous Koh-i-noor diamond, which was said to be the largest diamond in the world. When the British defeated the Sikhs in the Second Anglo-Sikh War, Dalip Singh was forced to surrender the Koh-i-noor diamond to Queen Victoria. This famous gem is still owned by the British royal family, but some Sikhs have campaigned to send it back to India.

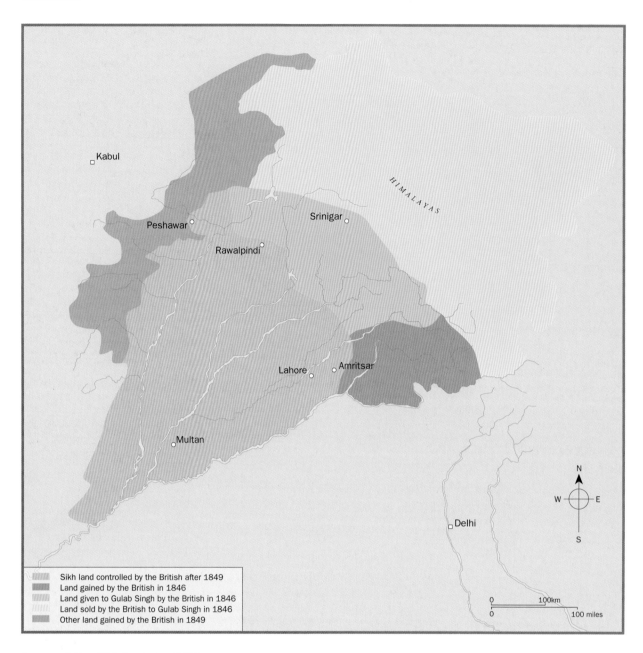

A map of the Sikh lands by 1850.

Key:
- Sikh land controlled by the British after 1849
- Land gained by the British in 1846
- Land given to Gulab Singh by the British in 1846
- Land sold by the British to Gulab Singh in 1846
- Other land gained by the British in 1849

After the wars Following the Second Anglo-Sikh War, the British took control of all Sikh lands. This takeover was called the Annexation of Punjab, or the Annexation of 1849. The British gained additional land in northwestern Punjab (see map) and also took control of central Punjab.

By June 1849, Punjab was divided into 27 districts, each run by a British administrator. The British collected taxes, ran the local police force and the courts, and tightly controlled all the local farms and industries.

In 1858, India became part of the British Empire, and the British increased their power within Punjab. The British built canals and railways, and Punjab became a flourishing area for farming and trade. The British also encouraged Sikhs to join the British army, rewarding Sikh soldiers with gifts of land.

Sikh unrest Although there were many examples of good relations between the Sikhs and the British, there were also problems. These were caused mainly by the British lack of understanding of Sikhism. For example, the British police controlled the grounds of the Golden Temple of Amritsar and allowed Hindus to place their idols there, even though this was against the Sikh religious law.

By the end of World War I (1914–18), there was also a growing feeling of unrest throughout India. An Indian nationalist movement began a campaign to free India from British rule. One of the leading figures in the nationalist movement was Mohandas Gandhi. He won many supporters among the Sikhs for his idea of a peaceful campaign for Indian independence.

The Massacre at Amritsar
On April 13, 1919, Sikh nationalists held a meeting in Jallianwala Bagh, an open plot of land close to the Golden Temple at Amritsar. This was also the day when the Sikhs celebrated their spring festival. Many families went to worship at the temple and then moved on to listen to the speeches at Jallianwala Bagh. It was a peaceful gathering, but it ended in tragedy for the Sikhs.

In the months leading up to this gathering, the British had begun to feel that their authority was threatened. When they heard of the nationalist meeting at Amritsar, the British authorities took action. On April 11, brigadier general Dyer arrived with his troops at Amritsar, and the following day, he declared all public meetings illegal. On the afternoon of April 13, Dyer learned that a large crowd had gathered at Jallianwala Bagh, and he ordered his troops to fire into the crowd. At least 379 men, women, and children were killed. People all over the world were horrified by the massacre. However, Dyer was not sorry. He later stated that his goal was to "strike terror . . . throughout the Punjab."

THE FESTIVAL OF BAISAKHI

On the day of the massacre at Amritsar, the Sikhs were celebrating Baisakhi. This festival to welcome spring was originally adopted from the Hindu religion. It also marks the Sikh New Year and the anniversary of the formation of the Khalsa by Guru Gobind Singh. Baisakhi is still celebrated by Sikhs today. At Baisakhi, the Nishan Sahib flag that flies outside each gurdwara is replaced with a new, clean flag. At the same time, the flagpole is washed in yogurt, a symbol of purity and cleanliness.

Sikhs take part in the annual spring festival of Baisakhi. The festival involves renewing the Sikh flag and washing the flagpole in yogurt to cleanse it for the coming year.

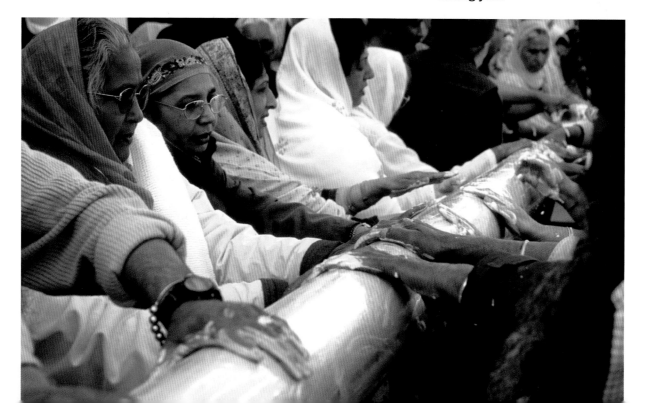

CHAPTER 4:
SIKHS IN THE TWENTIETH CENTURY

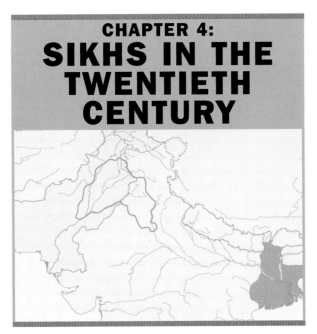

By the 1920s, the situation in Punjab was very tense. The Sikhs had not forgotten the massacre at Amritsar and many of them felt angry about British rule. Meanwhile, throughout India, Indians were campaigning for independence. At the same time, there were serious tensions between the Hindu and Muslim communities. The British often encouraged these arguments as a way of maintaining control in India.

Planning for partition

During the 1930s, the nationalist movement grew steadily, and people began to make plans for an independent India. However, the Muslims and Hindus could not agree on how to share the responsibility of governing India. In 1940, the Muslims demanded a separate Muslim country. This new country, to be called Pakistan, would include parts of Afghanistan and the western part of Punjab. It would be created by dividing the Sikh homeland right down the middle.

The Sikhs were bitterly opposed to the idea of Pakistan. To them, the division of Punjab meant the end of their dream of a united and independent Sikh state. In 1946, Sikh leaders presented their views to the Muslim leader, Mohammed Ali Jinnah. In this meeting, Jinnah proposed a plan to protect the Sikhs in the new Pakistan, but the Sikhs rejected Jinnah's offer.

The following day, the Sikhs made a dramatic statement to the Indian press. The newspaper headlines stated that Sikhs would never accept Pakistan. This public statement led to a series of riots in Punjab, as Muslims turned on Sikhs. However, in spite of these warnings of violence to come, the plans for partition continued. The Sikhs were a much smaller population than the Hindus and Muslims, so their views were easier to ignore.

The Partition of India

On August 14, 1947, the Partition of India took place and the new country of Pakistan was established. Pakistan was made up of two regions—West Pakistan and East Pakistan. The following day, India declared its independence from the United Kingdom. In the weeks and months that followed Partition, there were terrible massacres in West Pakistan as Muslims tried to drive Sikhs and Hindus out of their new country.

One of the many meetings held in 1947 to discuss the Partition of India. On the far left is the Sikh representative Sardar Baldev Singh. Leaning forward over the table is the future prime minister of India Jawaharlal Nehru.

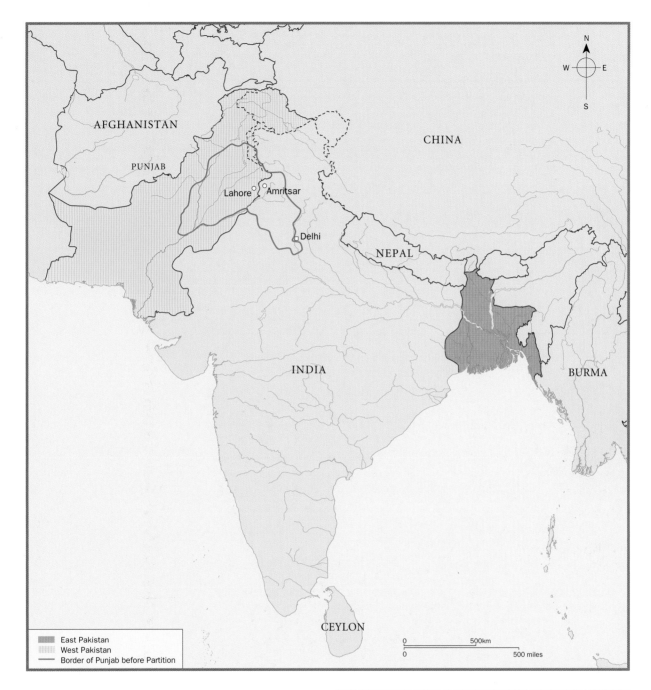

Legend:
- East Pakistan
- West Pakistan
- Border of Punjab before Partition

A map showing the Partition of India in 1947.

Thousands of Sikhs were driven from their homes, and many of their shrines and holy places were destroyed. Hundreds of thousands of Sikhs were killed, and nearly 40 percent of the Sikh community in India became refugees and had to rebuild their lives in a new land. Today, very few Sikhs live in Pakistan, and most of the Sikh holy places in the country are falling into ruin.

RESPECT FOR OTHER FAITHS

The first guru, Guru Nanak, taught that Sikhs should show respect to people of all religions. Despite their history of being persecuted by people of other faiths, most Sikhs follow this teaching. One way that Sikhs show respect is by welcoming people of all faiths into their gurdwaras and sharing a langar meal with them.

A map of the Punjab region after 1966.

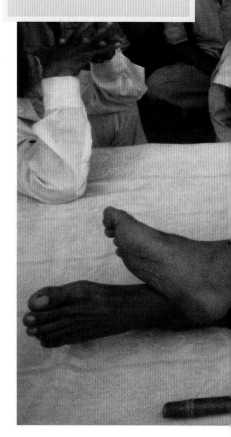

After Partition It took many years for the Sikh community to recover from the chaos of the Partition. But the Sikhs in East Punjab (the part of Punjab ruled by India) were determined to rebuild their lives, and by the end of the 1950s, agriculture was booming again. By the 1960s, East Punjab was India's main region for rice and wheat production.

While the people of East Punjab were working hard on their farms, other parts of India were advancing in different ways. These areas were benefiting from government aid to develop new industries. Many Sikhs felt they were being unfairly treated. They claimed the Indian government was treating Punjab as "the breadbasket of India," but not giving it the opportunity to modernize.

Carving up Punjab In 1966, the Indian government reorganized East Punjab into three separate districts called Himachal Pradesh, Haryana, and Punjab. Most of the Sikh holy shrines were in the new Punjab district, so this became the Sikh homeland, while the other districts had Hindu rulers. Once again, the Sikh territories were greatly reduced.

A voice of protest During the 1970s, a number of Sikhs became increasingly disillusioned with the Indian government. They were angry at the government's lack of support for industry and the way the Punjab region had been partitioned. Sikhs also resented the fact that they had so little power in Indian politics. Some Sikhs began to voice this anger in protest meetings. They demanded an independent state for the Sikhs, called Khalistan, based on the Khalsa—the community of Sikhs established by Guru Gobind Singh. There were also frequent clashes between Sikh and Hindu political groups.

One of the leading figures in the Sikh campaign for Khalistan was Jarnail Singh Bhindranwhale. He was a devout but fiery figure who believed that the Sikhs should be prepared to fight to the death for Khalistan. Bhindranwhale was violently opposed to the Indian government, led by Prime Minister Indira Gandhi. Gandhi, who was a skillful politician, allowed Bhindranwhale a lot of freedom. He appeared frequently on radio and TV and in the newspapers, and Indians came to believe that he represented all Sikhs. Many Indians feared that Bhindranwhale was preparing the Sikhs for a violent uprising.

In 1983, Bhindranwhale was accused of organizing violent opposition to the government. He was arrested briefly, then released. After this, he withdrew to the safety of the Golden Temple at Amritsar. Bhindranwhale and a group of followers locked themselves inside a building within the temple complex. They strengthened the building's defenses and armed themselves with a small stock of weapons. The stage was set for one of the most terrible events in Sikh history.

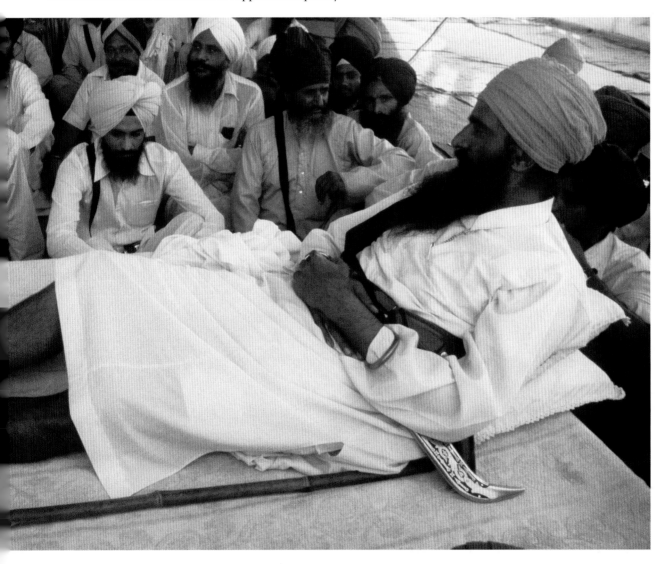

Jarnail Singh Bhindranwhale with a group of followers at the Golden Temple in Amritsar. Bhindranwhale believed that Sikhs should fight to the death for the chance to build their own nation.

Operation Bluestar

In the spring of 1984, a group of Sikh protestors decided to perform a symbolic act of defiance against the Indian government. In a public act of protest, they burned a page from the Indian constitution (the document outlining the government's laws). This was the opportunity that Prime Minister Gandhi had been waiting for. She began to plan for Operation Bluestar. Her plan was to arrest Bhindranwhale and prevent further resistance from the Sikhs.

In June 1984, Indian army tanks rolled into the temple complex at Amritsar, and Bhindranwhale and his followers were arrested. Many of the temple buildings were damaged and the Akal Takht was completely destroyed. The army also attacked 37 additional shrines across Punjab and killed thousands of Sikh males between the ages of 15 and 35. Altogether, more than 5,000 Sikhs died.

A terrible revenge

Operation Bluestar shocked and angered Sikhs throughout the world. In particular, they were furious that their holiest shrine had been attacked. On October 31, 1984, two Sikh bodyguards of the prime minister took their revenge and assassinated Mrs. Gandhi in the garden of her home.

Anti-Sikh riots

The assassination of Mrs. Gandhi sparked a further tide of violence against the Sikhs. All over northern India, Sikhs were attacked, and many were stabbed or burned alive. In Delhi, the riots lasted for four days and nights, and the government did not try to stop them.

The anti-Sikh riots had serious long-term consequences. The unrest created powerful militant groups among the Sikhs, who were prepared to use violence to achieve their goals. In the 1980s and 1990s, there were frequent clashes between Sikhs and Hindus. However, by the end of the twentieth century, the violence had subsided.

THE TEMPLE AT AMRITSAR

The two most important buildings in the temple complex at Amritsar are the Harimandir Sahib and the Akal Takht. The Harimandir Sahib, or holy shrine, was established in the sixteenth century by Guru Arjan. It is the holiest place in the Sikh religion and is the home of the original Guru Granth Sahib, the holy book of the Sikhs. Guru Arjan chose to build the Harimandir in the center of a lake, because the lake, or "pool of nectar," symbolizes the spiritual world. The Akal Takht was built by Guru Hargobind in the seventeenth century. Its name means "the Lord's almighty throne," and it is where the leaders of the Sikh faith meet to make decisions on various religious matters.

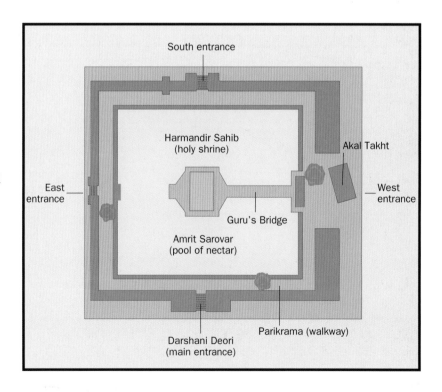

The floor plan of the temple complex at Amritsar.

Angry Sikhs riot in the streets of Amritsar in June 1984 to protest the presence of Indian troops in the Golden Temple.

CHAPTER 5: SIKHS AROUND THE WORLD

In the 1870s, Sikhs began to travel to different parts of the world. There was a shortage of land in Punjab, and consequently, not enough jobs. Many young men decided their best chance for a job was to search outside India. Some Sikhs moved abroad for a few years, and sent money home to their families before returning to India. Others settled permanently in their new countries.

Early emigrants Many of the early Sikh emigrants had been soldiers in the British army. In the 1870s, Sikh soldiers were sent overseas by the British. They were stationed in British colonies such as Malaya, Hong Kong, and Singapore. Later, they returned to

these countries to join the police force or work as security guards.

Sikhs also traveled to other parts of the British Empire. In the 1880s, many Sikhs left India for Australia. Some moved from there to New Zealand and the island of Fiji. However, Sikh emigration to Australia ended in the 1900s, when the country placed tougher restrictions on immigration.

Sikhs in Canada and the United States In 1897, several British regiments traveled through Canada to celebrate Queen Victoria's 50th anniversary on the British throne, her "Diamond Jubilee." Some of the Sikh soldiers in these regiments liked Canada and decided to emigrate. By the early 1900s, many Sikhs were settling in Canada, mainly working as lumberjacks.

Around this time, a few Sikhs also emigrated to the U.S. The first Sikh gurdwara in the U.S. was established in 1915 in Stockton, California. This simple temple was built beside the tracks of the Southern Pacific Railway. The Sikhs became well known for their charity, offering food and shelter to homeless people who walked along the railroad tracks.

By the 1920s, the Canadian and U.S. governments had placed strict restrictions on Sikh immigration. But by then, there were large Sikh settlements along the western coast of North America, especially in British Columbia, Washington, Oregon, and California.

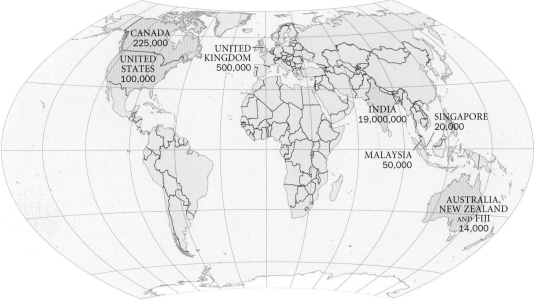

A map showing approximate number of Sikhs in various regions around the world today.

CANADA 225,000

UNITED STATES 100,000

UNITED KINGDOM 500,000

INDIA 19,000,000

SINGAPORE 20,000

MALAYSIA 50,000

AUSTRALIA, NEW ZEALAND AND FIJI 14,000

WESTERN SIKHS

In 1968, a Sikh spiritual teacher, Harbhajan Singh Puri, emigrated from India to Canada to teach yoga. He soon moved to California where he taught yoga to American students and explained the principles of Sikhism. Soon Harbhajan attracted a large group of people who wanted to follow his way of life. They became vegetarians and gave up alcohol, tobacco, drugs, and sex outside of marriage. They also spent part of every day meditating on the Sikh texts.

By the end of 1969, some of Harbhajan's students had entered the Sikh religion. These were the first of a growing number of Western Sikhs. Their movement is often known as 3HO, which stands for Healthy, Happy, Holy Organization. They wear white Punjabi clothing and turbans. Today, there are more than 10,000 Western Sikhs, mainly in the U.S.

A young American Sikh in northern New Mexico. The Western Sikh movement, or 3HO, is especially strong in the southwestern U.S.

Sikhs in Africa

Sikhs played an important role in the industrial development of East Africa. Between 1896 and 1901, Sikh carpenters, blacksmiths, and bricklayers traveled to Africa to help build the East African railways. After the railways were completed, many Sikhs remained in Africa and other Sikhs joined them there, working as farmers, civil servants, and policemen. In 1972, President Idi Amin expelled all Sikhs from Uganda. Some Ugandan Sikhs returned to India, but many chose to move to the UK.

Sikhs in the UK

The first Sikh emigrant to the UK was Maharaja Dalip Singh, the young Sikh ruler who lost his position as maharaja after the British won the Second Anglo-Sikh War. Dalip Singh visited Queen Victoria in 1854 and bought a grand house for himself. In 1911, the first gurdwara in the UK was built in London. More Sikhs arrived in the UK after World War I, but Sikh emigration greatly increased in the 1950s.

Sikh women prepare food in the kitchen of a British gurdwara. The UK was one of the first countries outside India to have a significant Sikh population.

LEARNING PUNJABI

Sikhs outside India form close-knit social groups. They meet regularly in their gurdwaras, which are both places of worship and social centers for the Sikh community. In the gurdwara, children learn to speak Punjabi and read and write its written form, Gurmukhi. Learning Punjabi allows young Sikhs to understand the teachings of their religion. It also gives them a strong link to the Sikh homeland in India.

Jats and non-Jats Two distinct groups of Sikhs have emerged in the UK. The early immigrants were mainly unskilled workers who had belonged to the Hindu untouchable caste in India. In the UK, Sikh immigrants often worked as traveling salesmen, selling merchandise from house to house. In the 1950s, a different group of Sikhs arrived in the UK. These people were known as Jats, people from farming families who owned land in India.

The Jats and non-Jats in the UK have often chosen to worship in separate gurdwaras. This division is also found in Sikh communities in other parts of the world. Many Sikhs are unhappy about the division because it goes against the teachings of Guru Nanak, who rejected the caste system and said that all people are equal.

A thriving religion Even though it was founded only 500 years ago, Sikhism is a major world religion. It is the world's fifth largest faith, after Christianity, Islam, Hinduism, and Buddhism. Today, there are more than 23 million Sikhs worldwide.

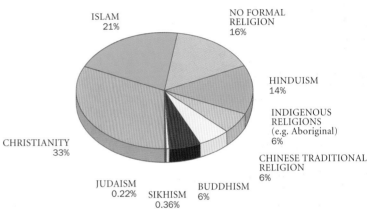

This pie chart shows the size of the world's Sikh population compared to other faiths.

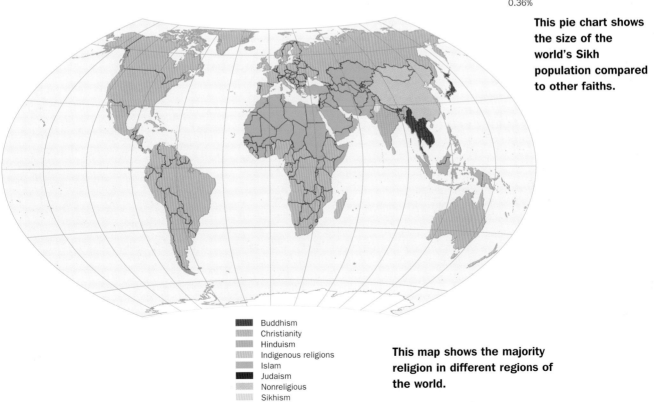

This map shows the majority religion in different regions of the world.

GREAT LIVES

Guru Nanak (1469–1539)

Guru Nanak was the founder of the Sikh religion and the first guru. He spent a large part of his life learning about other religions and considering the nature of God. He wrote his beliefs in a collection of hymns that formed the basis of the Sikh holy book, the Guru Granth Sahib. Nanak wrote these hymns in Gurmukhi, a written language that he created. He traveled widely, teaching his beliefs. Around 1520, he settled in Kartarpur and established the first Sikh community.

Guru Angad (1504–52)

Guru Angad became the second guru in 1539. He was a well educated man who collected Guru Nanak's hymns and added some of his own. He set up schools where young Sikhs could learn to read and write the Gurmukhi language. He also encouraged Sikhs to take part in regular sporting events.

Guru Amar Das (1479–1574)

Guru Amar Das was 73 when he became the third guru in 1552. He sent followers throughout Punjab to spread Sikhism. He also established a center for Sikhs at Goindwal, where he introduced the communal eating hall, known as the langar hall.

Guru Ram Das (1534–81)

Guru Ram Das became the fourth guru in 1574. He founded the city of Amritsar and worked to build the temple there. He also composed many hymns.

Guru Arjan (1563–1606)

Guru Arjan was the fifth guru. He succeeded his father in 1581. Guru Arjan was responsible for completing the temple at Amritsar. He also compiled the Adi Granth, a collection of Sikh holy writings. This would later be expanded to form the Guru Granth Sahib. Guru Arjan became the first Sikh martyr when he was tortured and killed by the Mogul emperor Jahangir.

Guru Hargobind (1595–1644)

Guru Hargobind was only 11 when he became the sixth guru in 1606, and he led the Sikhs for 38 years. Guru Hargobind prepared the Sikhs for war against the Moguls and led his army in some successful battles. He lived a wandering life, visiting Sikhs all over the Punjab region. Eventually, he settled in Kiratpur.

Guru Har Rai (1630–61)

Guru Har Raj became the seventh guru in 1644. He continued the military training of the Sikhs started by Guru Hargobind, but he did not engage in any serious battles. Guru Har Rai also began the practice of distributing medicine to the poor and sick.

Guru Har Krishan (1656–64)

Guru Har Krishan was a five-year-old child when he became the eighth guru. Three years later, he died of smallpox. Legend says that he offered water to other victims of the smallpox epidemic. Everyone who drank the water was cured, but the water could not save the young guru.

Guru Tegh Bahadur (1621–75)

In 1664, Guru Tegh Bahadur became the ninth guru. He traveled through northern India, visiting Sikhs, and also sharing ideas with members of other religions. In 1675, he stood bravely against the Mogul emperor Aurangzeb. He became the second Sikh martyr when he was tortured and killed for refusing to give up his beliefs.

Guru Gobind Singh (1666–1708)

Guru Gobind Singh became the tenth guru in 1675. He led the Sikhs in many battles. In 1699, he held a special ceremony to form the Khalsa, a group of devout Sikhs who were willing to die for their faith. Toward the end of his life, Guru Gobind Singh completed the Guru Granth Sahib. He died after being attacked by two Muslim assassins.

Banda Singh (1670–1716)

Banda Singh was a farmer, hunter, and warrior who decided to live a spiritual life practicing yoga. In 1708, he met Guru Gobind Singh and became a devoted Sikh. After the guru's death, Banda led the Sikhs in a series of daring raids and battles against the Moguls. He conquered large areas of land in southern Punjab and established a Sikh state. He is often known as "Banda Singh the Brave."

Bibi Anup Kaur (1690–1704)

Bibi Anup Kaur was a brave young woman. She joined the Khalsa soon after it was formed, trained a group of female warriors, and led them into battle against the Moguls. She also cooked and cared for Guru Gobind Singh on the battlefield. In 1704, she was captured, and a Mogul prince offered to marry her. But she killed herself so she would not be forced to convert to Islam. She was only 14 when she died.

Ranjit Singh (1780–1839)

Ranjit Singh was a brilliant horseman and warrior. At the age of 12, he succeeded his father as leader of a small territory in West Punjab. By the age of 18, he had united all the Sikh lands. By 19, Ranjit seized the city of Lahore from Muslim control. In 1801, Ranjit took the title of maharaja (prince). In the following years, he continued to acquire new lands. By the time he died, he had established a large Sikh kingdom. Ranjit modernized the army and was a fair ruler who treated all of his subjects equally and did not discriminate against other religions. His kingdom crumbled shortly after his death.

FACTS AND FIGURES

Approximate number of Sikhs worldwide

1960	6,000,000
1985	15,000,000
1990	20,000,000
2005	23,000,000

Approximate number of Sikhs in different regions of the world

Canada	225,000
United States	100,000
United Kingdom	500,000
India	19,000,000
Malaysia	50,000
Singapore	20,000
Australia, New Zealand, and Fiji	14,000

The symbols of the Khalsa

Sikhs who have taken part in the Khalsa ceremony, and become full members of their faith, wear the five symbols of the Khalsa to remind them of the promises they have made. These five symbols are often known as the 5 Ks. The 5 Ks date from the creation of the Khalsa by Guru Gobind Singh in 1699. Each symbol has a special significance.

- *kesh* (uncut hair)—This is a symbol of the Sikh devotion to God. Male Sikhs usually cover their hair with a turban.

- *kara* (a steel bangle)—The kara is worn on the right wrist. It is a symbol of the unity and equality of the Khalsa and a reminder of the eternal nature of God.

Festivals and Holy Days

Sikhs have two types of celebrations: *melas* and *gupurbs*. Melas are festivals. The three Sikh melas are Hola Mohalla, Baisakhi, and Divali. They each have their origins in Hindu festivals. Gupurbs are holy days that are held in honor of a Sikh guru. The four most commonly celebrated gupurbs are the birthdays of Guru Nanak and Guru Gobind Singh and the martyrdoms of Guru Arjan and Guru Tegh Bahadur. The anniversary of the installation of the Adi Granth in the Golden Temple is also a gupurb.

Month	Event
February/March	Hola Mohalla—the winter festival, when Sikhs hold sports competitions
May/June	Martyrdom of Guru Arjan
April	Baisakhi—the spring festival and the Sikh New Year, when Sikhs remember the forming of the Khalsa
October/November	Divali—the festival of lights Birthday of Guru Nanak
November/December	Martyrdom of Guru Tegh Bahadur
December	Birthday of Guru Gobind Singh

- *kangha* (a wooden comb)—The kangha is used by Sikhs to comb their hair. It symbolizes the discipline needed to develop the spiritual side of one's nature.

- *kachera* (cotton underwear)—The kachera symbolize the idea of modesty and of living a good life.

- *kirpan* (steel sword)—The kirpan was originally a real sword, but now it is a small, symbolic dagger. It represents the power and freedom found in the Sikh faith.

Sikh Services

Sikh services can last for many hours. Services include readings from the Guru Granth Sahib. They also include Kirtan, the Ardas prayer, and the sharing of Karah Parshad.

- Kirtan—Singing hymns accompanied by musicians.

- The Ardas—The final prayer in Sikh services and ceremonies. It encourages Sikhs to remember their gurus and asks for God's blessing on the Sikh community and all people everywhere.

- Karah Parshad—At the end of all Sikh services and ceremonies, Karah Parshad is served. It is made from a mixture of flour (or semolina), ghee (clarified butter), and sugar. Karah Parshad is a sign of the gurus' blessings on everyone.

FURTHER INFORMATION

Books

Religions of the World: Sikhism by Sewa Singh Kalsi (Chelsea House Publications, 2005)

Sikhism: A New Approach by Pamela Draycott (Hodder Murray, 1996)

The Sikhs by Patwant Singh (Image, 2001)

Teach Yourself Sikhism by Owen Cole (McGraw-Hill, 2005)

Web sites

www.allaboutsikhs.com
A large Web site devoted to Sikhism. Includes pages on Sikh history, Sikh beliefs, and the Sikh way of life.

www.sikhs.org
A well-organized site on the Sikh religion, with useful graphics.

www.sikhiwiki.org
An online Sikh encyclopedia.

www.sikh-history.com
A Web site on Sikh history. Contains sections on gurus, warriors, martyrs, and modern Sikh personalities.

DVDs

Gandhi (1982)
This feature film about the life of Mohandas Gandhi has become a classic. It includes scenes of the massacre at Amritsar and the events that followed the Partition of India.

TIME LINE

1469	Guru Nanak, the first guru, is born in Punjab.
ca.1520	Guru Nanak establishes the first Sikh community in Kartarpur.
1526	The Moguls seize control of Delhi.
1539	Guru Angad becomes the second guru.
1552	Guru Amar Das becomes the third guru.
1574	Guru Ram Das becomes the fourth guru.
1581	Guru Arjan becomes the fifth guru.
1604	The temple at Amritsar is completed.
1606	Guru Arjan is tortured and put to death by the Mogul emperor Jahangir. Guru Hargobind becomes the sixth guru.
1631	The Sikhs defeat the Moguls at the Battle of Lahira.
1634	The Sikhs defeat the Moguls at the battle of Kartarpur.
1644	Guru Har Rai becomes the seventh guru.
1661	Guru Har Krishan becomes the eighth guru.
1664	Guru Tegh Bahadur becomes the ninth guru.
1675	Guru Tegh Bahadur is tortured and put to death by the Mogul emperor, Aurangzeb. Guru Gobind Singh becomes the tenth guru.
1699	Guru Gobind Singh forms the Khalsa.
ca.1706	Guru Gobind Singh completes the Guru Granth Sahib.
1708	Guru Gobind Singh dies from an attack by Muslim assassins. Banda Singh begins to seize land from the Moguls.
1715	Banda Singh is defeated by the Moguls.
1801	Ranjit Singh declares himself maharaja of the Punjab.
1809	Ranjit Singh signs the Treaty of Amritsar with the British.
1845	The First Anglo-Sikh War begins.
1846	The First Anglo-Sikh War ends in victory for the British. The Sikhs and the British sign the Treaty of Lahore.
1848	Sikhs rise up against the British in the Multan Revolt. The Second Anglo-Sikh War begins.
1849	The Second Anglo-Sikh War ends in victory for the British. The British take over all the Sikh lands.
1858	India becomes part of the British Empire.
1870s	Sikh emigration begins.
1914	World War I begins. Many Sikhs fight in the British army.
1919	The Massacre at Amritsar.
1939	World War II begins. Many Sikhs fight in the British army.
1947	The Partition of India and Indian Independence.
1966	The Punjab region is divided into three states.
1969	Harbhajan Singh Puri founds the 3HO in California.
1984	Indira Gandhi launches Operation Bluestar against the Sikhs. Two Sikhs assassinate Mrs. Ghandi and there are many anti-Sikh riots.
2005	There are more than 23 million Sikhs worldwide.

GLOSSARY

Adi Granth A Sikh holy book compiled by Guru Arjan. It contains hymns written by the gurus and some writings by Muslim and Hindu holy men.

assassinate Murder an important person.

bhakti movement A branch of Hinduism. Bhaktis ignore the caste system and concentrate on devotion to a personal god.

Buddhism A religion based on the teachings of the Buddha. Buddhists believe that they should not become too attached to material things and that they will live many lives in different bodies.

caste system A system of grouping people in separate classes (or castes). The caste system began in ancient India, but it has now almost completely disappeared.

colony A country or area that is ruled by another country and has been settled by people from the ruling country.

communal Shared.

compile Bring together many pieces of information.

constitution A document that contains the laws by which a country is governed.

devout Deeply religious.

emigrant Someone who leaves his or her own country and settles in a new land.

expel Drive someone out.

gurdwara A place where the Guru Granth Sahib is kept and where Sikhs go to worship.

guru In Sikhism and Hinduism, a religious leader or teacher.

Guru Granth Sahib The Sikh holy book, which is regarded as a guru.

Hinduism The main religion of India. Hindus worship many gods and believe that they will live many lives in different bodies.

horoscope A prediction about someone's life, based on the position of the stars and planets at the time of his or her birth.

hymn A song of praise to God.

immigrant Someone who comes to a new country from abroad and permanently settles there.

installed Put something in place.

Islam A religion based on the teachings of the Prophet Muhammed.

langar The food that is served to everyone who comes to a gurdwara.

lumberjack Someone who cuts down trees to sell as lumber.

maharaja An Indian prince.

meditate Think very deeply about something.

mosque A building where Muslims go to worship.

mystical Connected with the spirit rather than the body.

nationalist Someone who is very proud of his or her country. Nationalists are often prepared to fight for their country.

partition The dividing of something into two or more parts.

refugee A person who has been forced to leave his or her home because of war or some other disaster.

regiment A large group of soldiers in an army.

scholar A highly educated person.

sewa The Sikh duty of service to others.

stationed Based somewhere for a while, usually during service in the military.

succeed Take over a position from someone else.

Sufism A branch of Islam. Sufis lead a very simple life and meditate on the nature of God.

INDEX